2024

NASHVILLE

INSIDER TRIP

Travel Guide

VIDEO & AUDIO LIFE STORY TRIP BONUS

MAP INCLUDED

Myers Brooks

Nashville Travel Guide

2024

Budget-friendly Travel Tips, Brief History,Culinary Delights, Top Attractions, Restaurants, Must Visit Cities to Explore in Tennessee.

SAFE TRIP
TRAVEL ITINERARY

Myers Brooks

Table of Content

SAFE TRIP
TRAVEL ITINERARY

Scan Qr Code to Navigate your way in Nashville,Tennessee.

INTRODUCTION

Nashville, **Tennessee,** is unquestionably the Music City, a seamless fusion of rich history and cutting-edge innovation. Without a doubt, Nashville, Tennessee, is the Music City—a seamless blend of innovative technology and historic heritage.

Everyone who comes Nashville is enthralled with this vibrant city. Nashville's beat welcomes you with open arms the instant you arrive.

This upbeat urban tune is made up of more than only its well-known status in the country music scene.

The air is filled with the sound of strumming guitars, heartfelt melodies from street performers, and a true Southern welcome that is in line with the city's rich musical heritage. Here, among the neon signs and historic buildings, come the inspiration for aspiring composers as well as well-known performers.

The heartbeat of Nashville's music culture is found in the live music clubs and honky-tonks that line Broadway. Each has a distinct history and a soundtrack that bleeds into the pavements. Here, music acts as a universal language, bringing people from all origins together.

Whatever your interests—food, travel, or music—*Nashville assures you of an incredible experience that will stick in your head long after the last note fades.*

CHAPTER 1

WELCOME TO NASHVILLE MUSIC CITY

The Ryman Auditorium, dubbed the "**Mother Church of Country Music**," provides an almost spiritual experience for music enthusiasts, while the Grand Ole Opry, the longest-running radio show in the world, continues to showcase the best in country music.

Nashville's music, though, isn't just country. The musical landscape of the city is varied, encompassing Americana, pop, rock, blues, and pop. Beyond the music, Nashville's food industry is a crescendo of sensations. The

Bluebird Cafe, nestled away in a suburban shopping mall, is a monument to the city's love for songwriting, where hit-makers and hopefuls share their stories in an intimate setting.

In addition to posh restaurants and creative chefs pushing the boundaries of traditional Southern cuisine to create a gourmet paradise as varied as its music, hot chicken, a local delicacy, delivers a scorching taste of the city's character. The city's many museums and galleries are further examples of its rich cultural heritage.

The Country Music Hall of Fame and **Museum** has interactive exhibitions and a vast collection of items that document the history of the genre. In the meanwhile, Nashville's varied creative community is reflected in the exhibitions of the Frist Art Museum, which is situated in an impressive Art Deco edifice and features pieces from across the world to the local.

The city's highlights are its festivals and events, which range from the internationally renowned CMA Music Festival to regional celebrations of cuisine, art, and community. Nashville's open areas provide a counterbalance to its metropolitan pulse. These events highlight the city's ability to combine its musical origins with a forward-thinking and inclusive attitude.

The Cumberland River beckons outdoor enthusiasts to explore its waters, and parks like Centennial Park, with its full-scale reproduction of the Parthenon, provide a tranquil haven. Education and innovation also play major roles in Nashville's makeup. The city's enterprising and educated attitude is fueled by renowned colleges and a growing tech sector, which keeps the chorus dynamic.

The city's skyline, a silhouette against the Tennessee sky as dusk draws in, is a striking image of its dual identity—boldly contemporary yet deeply rooted in history. The modern high-rises in the downtown area and the elegant Victorian mansions in Germantown both reflect a city that is anxious to write its future while honoring its history.

Every face, every street, and every corner in Nashville has a tale to tell—a song just waiting to be heard. This city extends an invitation for you to participate in its continuous symphony, listen, and explore. Nashville offers a trip that will have you singing its song long after you've left, whether you're here for the cuisine, art, music, or just the whole experience.

Essentially, **Nashville is an experience**, a way of life, and a community that is nourished by the rhythm of existence rather than just a travel destination. It's a city that needs to be experienced—it feels like home, no matter where you are from. *Greetings from Music City, where each visit is a note in Nashville's big melody.*

CHAPTER 2

Why Visit Nashville?

Over time, Nashville has changed and developed into a city that offers a wide range of experiences to a diverse range of visitors. It's a well-liked weekend retreat for people from the Midwest and East Coast. For those who enjoy both foreign fusion and reasonably priced Southern cooking, it's a culinary haven.

It's also a great place for friends to get together before making the huge decision to be married, whether they are bachelors or bachelorettes. But at its core, Nashville is a sanctuary for lovers of country music. Some of the best unknown musicians in the nation may be found performing in the taverns along Broadway, as well as in the well-known Bluebird Cafe, which is located around five miles south.

Many performers, including **Faith Hill, Tim McGraw, Reba McEntire, Taylor Swift, Florida Georgia Line, and Sam Hunt**, were really found or got their start in music in Nashville. Taking advantage of the free live music offered at various locations around the city is the ideal way to see Nashville's country culture.

In addition, you ought go see The Parthenon, take a tour of Belle Meade Historic Site, and visit the Grand Ole Opry and the Country Music Hall of Fame. Additionally, schedule some time to simply relax at one of the many restaurants, coffee shops, and boutiques that are opening up downtown.

Nashville is a veritable melting pot of interesting things! If you enjoy music, this area is truly paradise. There are a ton of fantastic pubs and live music venues, particularly on Broadway. There's some incredible potential to be found, who knows, the next great star!

There are many other genres of music available here, not only country. Additionally, you may learn everything there is to know about Nashville's musical history at well-known locations like the Grand Ole Opry and the Country Music Hall of Fame.

But music isn't the only thing in Nashville. There are also many interesting historical sites to see, such as The Parthenon and Belle Meade Historic Site. Additionally, there are tons of hip stores, cafés, and eateries to check out in downtown.

There are parks and lakes where you may go hiking, biking, or just relax in the great outdoors if you're an outdoor enthusiast. Furthermore, Nashville is the ideal destination for foodies. You may sample a wide variety of delectable Southern fare as well as elegant fusion meals.

Music culture: Nashville is well-known for its Broadway-area live music culture. You may go down the street and enter any pub to see excellent musicians performing a variety of genres, such as pop, rock, country, and blues.

For small-scale concerts by emerging songwriters, the Bluebird Cafe is a must-go-to venue. Enjoy the Grand Ole Opry as well, a historic location that has been home to famous country music concerts for almost a century.

Another must-see is the Country Music Hall of Fame, which has displays tracing the evolution and influence of the genre from its beginnings to contemporary celebrities.

Historical Sites: Belle Meade Historic Site provides guided tours of the home and gardens, providing insight into Nashville's former plantation life. The Parthenon, a full-scale reproduction of the ancient Greek structure with an art museum within, is situated in Centennial Park.

Explore Downtown: There are many of stores, cafés, and restaurants to discover in Nashville's vibrant downtown. You may stroll along Honky Tonk Highway, also known as Lower Broadway, to take in the vibrant atmosphere and see live music performances. While you're downtown, make sure to sample some traditional Southern fare like hot chicken or barbecue.

Outdoor Adventures: With parks, trails, and lakes to explore, Nashville has an abundance of outdoor leisure possibilities. Miles of hiking and biking paths may be found at Shelby Bottoms Nature Center and Greenway, while Centennial Park is a well-liked location for picnics and leisurely walks. For water sports like fishing and boating, Percy Priest Lake is ideal.

Nashville's rich culinary culture reflects the city's multicultural influences, making it a food lover's heaven. At one of the numerous restaurants in the city, you may indulge in classic Southern fare like fried chicken and biscuits or enjoy some creative fusion food. Remember to wash it all down with a cool glass of sweet tea or a craft beer that was made nearby.

All things considered, Nashville has plenty to offer everyone, regardless of your interests—music, history, outdoor recreation, or cuisine. It is understandable why Nashville is such a well-liked travel destination for tourists of all ages given its energetic environment and wide range of activities!

ABOUT THIS GUIDE

Your pass to the greatest of Nashville's colorful and varied offers is this guide. This book is intended to give you useful insights, advice, and suggestions to help you make the most of your stay in Nashville, regardless of whether you're a first-time visitor or an experienced tourist eager to explore Music City in greater detail.

Inside, you'll discover comprehensive details on Nashville's music culture, including must-see locations, important historical sites, and insider advice on how to enjoy live shows like a native. Along with that, we'll take you on a gastronomic tour of Nashville's many dining options, which range from inventive fusion meals to classic Southern foods.

However, **Nashville is a city rich in history**, culture, and outdoor activities in addition to its cuisine and music. Discover the hidden treasures that make Music City unique as you explore Nashville's exciting historical landmarks, lively neighborhoods, and picturesque parks with the aid of this book.

With everything you need to make your trip to Nashville unique, this book is perfect whether you're planning a solo adventure, a family vacation, or a weekend break. So prepare to discover all Music City has to offer, grab your cowboy boots, and get going!

Advantages of This Reference:

Insider Advice: Get access to advice and suggestions from seasoned tourists and locals, which can help you find hidden treasures and make the most of your trip to Nashville.

Extensive Coverage: This book covers every facet of Nashville, from the thriving music scene to the rich cultural legacy, making sure you don't miss any of the must-see sights and activities in the area.

Practical Information: You may easily plan and navigate your trip to Nashville with confidence by finding useful information on lodging alternatives, transportation, and other important travel recommendations.

Personalized Suggestions: Whether you're an outdoor explorer, a foodie, or a music lover, this book provides recommendations specifically catered to your interests, making sure you have a rewarding and unforgettable time in Music City.

Time-saving: By using this guide, you can quickly take advantage of all Nashville has to offer instead of spending hours researching and preparing, which will save you time and trouble when traveling.

Memorable Experiences: You may make lifelong memories and experiences by heeding the advice and recommendations in this book, which will guarantee that your vacation to Nashville is genuinely unique and fruitful.

The Best Times to Go to Nashville

April through **October** are the ideal months to visit Nashville because of the pleasant weather that makes this music metropolis come alive. Winter is low season, however December is particularly attractive with the **Opryland Hotel** and the Belle Meade Historic Site decked out for Christmas. You might be able to get somewhat cheaper airfares and accommodation prices from **November to March.**

Spring: *March to May*
Nashville is especially beautiful in the spring, when trees and vibrant flowers bloom all across the city.

With average highs and lows in the 50s to 70s Fahrenheit (**10 to 25 degrees Celsius**), the weather is generally pleasant, which makes it perfect for outdoor pursuits like bicycling, hiking, and seeing the city's parks and gardens.

You may take part in activities like the Nashville Film Festival and the Nashville Earth Day Festival in addition to the Nashville Cherry Blossom Festival, which commemorates the coming of spring with live music, food trucks, and cherry blossom gazing.

Plus, spring offers a more laid-back and private setting for touring and sightseeing because there are less tourists than in the summer.

Autumnal (September–November):

Fall is a great season to visit Nashville because of the city's brilliant fall foliage and pleasanter weather. Hiking, apple picking, and outdoor events are all made possible by the ideal weather, which reaches highs in the 60s and 70s Fahrenheit **(15–25 degrees Celsius).**

The Nashville Oktoberfest provides a taste of German culture with beer samples, live music, and food vendors, while the September Americana Music Festival features the best in Americana and roots music. Fall foliage drives are particularly well-liked as they give you a chance to take in Tennessee's breathtaking rural scenery as the trees change color.

June to August is summer:
Nashville experiences hot, muggy summers that frequently reach highs of 80 and 90

degrees Fahrenheit (**over 30 degrees Celsius**). Summer is a busy season in the city despite the heat, with outdoor activities such as festivals and concerts taking place practically every weekend.

For aficionados of country music, the June CMA Music Festival is a highlight as it features concerts by prominent performers on several stages located around downtown Nashville. Thousands of music enthusiasts from all over the world congregate to the nearby Bonnaroo Music and Arts Festival for four days of camping, music, and camaraderie.

Even though it can become quite hot, there are many of ways to remain cool, including going to splash parks and water parks or taking advantage of indoor activities like theaters and museums.

Winter: *January to February*

Compared to other sections of the nation, Nashville experiences a somewhat warm winter, with average highs in the 30s to 50s Fahrenheit *(0–15 degrees Celsius)*. Snowfall

is infrequent, but when the holidays roll around, the city turns into a shimmering wonderland complete with Christmas decorations, sparkling lights, and festive festivities.

A Country Christmas at Gaylord Opryland Resort and the Nashville Flea Market provide distinctive shopping experiences, while the Nashville Christmas Parade, which takes place in December, includes Santa Claus, marching bands, and floats.

Live music concerts are held indoors all winter long at venues like the Grand Ole *Opry and the Ryman Auditorium,* offering visitors a warm haven from the cold. Winter is a terrific time to visit Nashville's museums, galleries, and eateries without the crowds because there are less tourists than during other seasons.

REQUIREMENTS FOR TRAVEL

There are a few prerequisites that must be met before visiting Nashville:

Transport:

Nashville International Airport (BNA) is the main airport for visitors arriving by air. It is situated around southeast of Nashville's downtown. Large airlines provide daily flights to and from locations around the United States and abroad, providing both local and international flight options from the airport.

Driving: Major interstate routes like as I-65, I-40, and I-24 make it simple to reach Nashville if you're going by automobile. There is parking everywhere throughout the city, including on public spaces, in garages, and on streets.

Public Transportation: Bus services are offered by Nashville's public transportation system, the Nashville Metropolitan Transit Authority (MTA), across the city and its environs. Furthermore, ride-sharing services such as Uber and Lyft are extensively accessible for easy mobility across Nashville.

Accommodation:

Nashville has a wide selection of lodging choices to fit every taste and budget. There is lodging for all budgets and tastes, ranging from boutique bed and breakfasts and opulent hotels to affordable motels and vacation rentals.

The Gulch, East Nashville, Midtown, and downtown Nashville are popular areas to stay in. Since hotels and rental houses tend to fill up quickly, make sure to book your accommodations well in advance, especially if you're going during busy seasons or important events.

Spending limit:

For your vacation to Nashville, you should plan a budget in order to make sure you can afford to take advantage of everything the city has to offer.

When making your budget, take into account things like the cost of lodging, travel expenditures, eating out, entertainment, and souvenir purchasing. Remember that costs might change according on the season, demand, and degree of luxury you choose.

You may maximize your Nashville experience while staying inside your budget by doing pricing research and establishing reasonable spending boundaries.

Events and Attractions:

Nashville offers a huge selection of attractions and events for people of all ages and interests. Everyone can find something to enjoy, regardless of their interests—music lovers, history buffs, foodies, or outdoor enthusiasts.

Making the most of your time in Nashville will enable you to prioritize your must-see locations and plan ahead for attractions and activities. To minimize disappointment, think about buying tickets or making reservations ahead of time, particularly for well-liked tours, performances, and attractions.

Guidelines for COVID-19:

Before traveling to Nashville, it's essential to check the latest COVID-19 guidelines and restrictions, as they may vary depending on local conditions and government regulations.

To protect yourself and others during your visit, be ready to adhere to health and safety regulations, which include wearing masks, using social distancing techniques, and often washing your hands.

Keep yourself updated on any special rules or specifications that apply to the attractions, locations, and events you want to attend. These establishments could have their own policies in place to protect both visitors and employees.

To add to your peace of mind during your journey to Nashville, think about getting travel insurance that covers COVID-19-related costs like medical care and trip cancellations.

Chapter 3:

A Tour of the Neighborhoods of Nashville

Nashville's Downtown: *The City's Pulse*

The center of activity in Nashville is downtown, which is comparable to the city's beating heart. It's a location where the rush of excitement, the brightness of neon lights, and the sound of music fill the streets. Imagine yourself strolling along Broadway, the major thoroughfare, with bars and honky-tonks all around you with live music pouring out onto the pavements.

It's possible to witness a budding artist in action at renowned locations such as The Stage or Tootsie's Orchid Lounge.

However, downtown Nashville is home to a plethora of culture and history in addition to music. Music enthusiasts should not miss the Ryman Auditorium, also referred to as the **"Mother Church of Country Music,"** because of its famed stage, which has played host to many memorable concerts. You may also tour the Tennessee State Museum and take in the artwork of the Frist Art Museum to learn more about Tennessee's rich past.

The John Seigenthaler Pedestrian Bridge provides expansive views of the metropolitan skyline and the serene waters of the Cumberland River for those looking for a moment of serenity amid the activity. It's the ideal location for a relaxed stroll or a picturesque picture opportunity.

And let's not overlook the cuisine! With delectable meals to satiate every appetite, downtown Nashville is a gastronomic haven. There is plenty to entice every appetite, from melt-in-your-mouth barbecue to blazing hot chicken and comforting Southern comfort cuisine.

Rich in personality and imagination, East Nashville attracts a diverse mix of creative types, musicians, and free spirits. *A closer look at what makes this place so special is provided here:*

<u>Vibrant Street Art & old Charm</u>: When you first arrive in East Nashville, you'll be struck by the colorful murals that paint many of the neighborhood's old brick buildings. The area is given vitality by vibrant murals that capture its spirit of creativity and feeling of communal pride. Every painting celebrates the neighborhood's many cultures and rich history by telling a different tale.

Funky Boutiques and Art Galleries: Offering a treasure trove of one-of-a-kind treasures and handcrafted products, East Nashville is home to an eclectic mix of boutiques and art galleries. There are many of places to explore and buy, from eccentric gift shops and antique apparel stores to modern art galleries featuring local talent.

Every customer will find something to love in East Nashville, whether they are looking for a unique memento or are just perusing the selection for ideas.

Chic Restaurants and Handcrafted Coffee: East Nashville's thriving culinary scene and handcrafted coffee culture draw in foodies and coffee connoisseurs alike. There are several contemporary restaurants in the neighborhood that provide inventive food, as well as quaint cafés that serve fine brunch fare. There are many possibilities to sate your appetite, whether it's for a sumptuous dessert, a farm-to-table feast, or a delectable burger.

And a trip to East Nashville wouldn't be complete without savoring a cup of expertly made gourmet coffee from nearby roasters.

Live Performances in Small locations: East Nashville is a neighborhood where music is deeply ingrained, with live events taking place in various tiny locations. You can find a show and discover fresh talent everywhere you go, from little coffee shops and dive bars to ancient theaters and music halls.

Both locals and visitors may enjoy an immersive and genuine musical experience as local artists perform on stage and display their talents. There's something for every kind of music lover in East Nashville, including folk, blues, rock, and indie.

The Gulch: Contemporary Charm and Urban Renewal

Like the hip and happening portion of Nashville, The Gulch is where it's all at. It has towering, sleek, modern buildings with chic stores and upscale dining options. However, the truly remarkable thing about The Gulch is how it blends the modern with the ancient.

You'll witness modern skyscrapers that contrast sharply with the skyline and converted ancient warehouses into posh flats.

The Gulch offers a ton of activities in addition to its attractive appearance. Shopping in the hip shops, having a bite to eat at one of the upscale eateries, or seeing a movie at the upscale theater may occupy your entire day.

The Gulch is essentially the place to go if you want to feel like you're right in the midst of everything, surrounded by hip stores, interesting architecture, and plenty of activities. It's the ideal spot to hang out with friends and experience the best area in Nashville's hipster culture.

Germantown: Art Deco Buildings and Gourmet Eats

Nashville's Germantown is like traveling back in time. It's the oldest area in the city and well-known for its gorgeous ancient buildings and quaint cobblestone streets. Imagine centuries-old structures with fascinating histories and tastefully

decorated Victorian residences. You may stroll about here and get the impression that you are in a different time period.

But Germantown is more than simply a picturesque area; it's a culinary lover's dream come true. There are a ton of fantastic eateries in this area that provide a wide variety of delectable dishes. You'll find something to please your palate, ranging from cuisines from around the world to fresh, farm-to-table food. Germantown offers everything you could possibly want, whether you're craving a luxury supper or a fast lunch.

Germantown also offers culture, if that's your thing. Visit galleries featuring the creations of regional artists or take in a performance at the Germantown Performing Arts Center. It's an area rich in history and vitality, making it the ideal spot for exploration and new learning experiences.

Chapter 4

Entertainment and Music

Historic Locations: *Highlights of Nashville's Music Scene*

Some of the most storied music venues in the world, each with its own distinct charm and history, can be found in Nashville. These locations, which include the legendary Grand Ole Opry, where country music icons have played for decades, and the historic Ryman Auditorium, dubbed the "**Mother Church of Country Music**," are an essential part of Nashville's musical history.

A trip to Music City would not be complete without taking in live music at one of these iconic venues, whether you're seeing a Grammy-winning performer or discovering a new artist.

Ryman Auditorium: *Nashville's #2 Ryman AuditoriumThe city center is 0.2 kilometers away. Address: 116 Fifth Ave.*

The Ryman Auditorium, sometimes referred to as the "**Mother Church of Country Music**," is one of Nashville's most recognizable and significant performance spaces.

Originally constructed in 1892 as a tabernacle, the Ryman rose to prominence as the Grand Ole Opry's home from 1943 until 1974, when stars like Hank Williams, Patsy Cline, and Johnny Cash gave unforgettable performances.

Top performers from various genres, including rock, pop, and Americana, still visit the Ryman today because of its outstanding acoustics and extensive history. Explore displays featuring artifacts from the Ryman's historic musical heritage and learn about the venue's legendary past with guided tours.

Grand Ole Opry: Nashville's top grand old operaThe city center is six kilometers away. Address: 2804 Opryland Drive Nightlife & Entertainment, Touring

One of the most prestigious establishments in the country music industry, the Grand Ole Opry was first established as a radio program in 1925.

The Grand Ole Opry House, where it now resides and continues to present the finest in country music, replaced the Ryman Auditorium as the venue for the Opry in 1974.

Fans of country music should not miss the Opry stage, which has hosted several renowned singers throughout the years, such as Dolly Parton, Garth Brooks, and Carrie Underwood.

Visitors may explore the Opry House's rich history and behind-the-scenes operations in addition to seeing live concerts.

Bluebird Cafe:

Even though the Bluebird Cafe is tiny, it has a significant impact on Nashville's music industry as a top location for singer-songwriters.

Nestled in an unremarkable strip center, the Bluebird rose to prominence as a platform for emerging songwriters, playing small-scale shows with stars like **Kathy Mattea, Garth Brooks, and Taylor Swift.**

Because of the venue's "in the round" layout, songwriters may play their original works in a small, intimate environment, giving listeners a one-of-a-kind and unforgettable experience.

Securing tickets to an event at the Bluebird might be difficult due to its tiny size and popularity, but the opportunity to see unadulterated talent up close makes the effort worthwhile.

Not only are these iconic locations great places to attend shows, but they also serve as living tributes to Nashville's rich musical history and its ongoing status as "**Music City, USA**." Whether you're a casual listener or a devoted fan, seeing live music at one of these legendary venues is a must-do when visiting Nashville.

Scene for Live Music: *From Concert Halls to Honky Tonks*

In Nashville, music permeates every aspect of the city, from the Lower Broadway honkytonks to the numerous theaters and concert venues. You may visit any bar on Broadway and witness live music performed by skilled musicians, or you can go to one of Nashville's concert halls to see a top-tier performer take the stage.

Nashville's thriving live music culture has something for every music fan to enjoy, with styles ranging from blues and jazz to country and rock.

Downtown Honky-Tonks on Broadway:

With neon lights, live music spilling out into the streets, and a vibrant environment that draws both residents and tourists, Lower Broadway is the core of Nashville's honky-tonk culture.

Traditional pubs known for their emphasis on country music, honky-tonks have excellent bands and performers that play all day and into the night.

Hikers may explore Lower Broadway, stopping at several honky-tonks to experience the vibrant atmosphere of Music City and try out various bands.

Several well-known honky-tonks with distinct histories and charms are Tootsie's Orchid Lounge, Robert's Western World, and The Stage.

Theaters and concert halls:

Nashville is home to several theaters and concert venues that provide performances by top performers in a variety of genres.

Nashville's main classical music venue, the Schermerhorn Symphony Center, is also home to the Grammy-winning Nashville Symphony Orchestra.

With more than 20,000 seats, the Bridgestone Arena is a sizable indoor venue that frequently holds big concerts and events.

During the summer months, prominent performers perform at the Ascend

Amphitheater, an outdoor venue by the Cumberland River that offers stunning views of the Nashville cityscape.

Other noteworthy locations that provide a distinctive musical experience are the Grand Ole Opry House, the historic Exit/In, and the Ryman Auditorium.

Variety of Genres:

Nashville's live music industry is known for its diverse spectrum of genres, which appeals to a broad audience's musical preferences.

In Music City, country music reigns supreme, but there are other places that feature rock, blues, jazz, Americana, gospel, and other genres.

Whether you're a devoted fan or simply trying something new, there's something for everyone to appreciate, from cozy acoustic settings to exciting rock shows.

Nightly performances by a variety of venues with changing artist lineups guarantee that Nashville's live music scene is constantly interesting and new.

In conclusion, honky-tonks, theaters, and concert halls in Nashville offer a diverse range of sounds and experiences for live music enthusiasts, making the city's live music scene a dynamic tapestry. You'll be engrossed in Music City, USA's rich musical history whether you're taking in a symphony at the Schermerhorn or dancing the night away on Lower Broadway.

Music History Tours: *Following the Musical Heritage of Nashville*

Taking a music history tour is the best way to fully immerse yourself in Nashville's rich musical heritage. A fascinating look into Nashville's rich musical history can be had on these excursions, which range from immersive experiences at museums and recording studios to guided walking tours of iconic music monuments.

Discover the background of some of the most well-known songs and performers in country, rock, and blues music, as well as the influence the city had on these genres.

Walking Tours with a Guide:
Walking tours led by guides provide an overview of Nashville's rich musical history while taking guests on a tour of the city's most famous music sites.
Typically, these trips go through historic districts like Music Row, where guests may

view landmark venues where great musicians recorded their songs as well as recording studios and music publishing organizations.

In-depth guides provide Nashville's musical heritage perspective and nuance by sharing tales and anecdotes about the city's influence on the country, rock, and blues music scenes.

It is possible for tourists to follow in the footsteps of music icons by going to the locations where famous songs were composed, recorded, and performed.

Immersion-Based Activities:

Visitors may enter Nashville's legendary past with immersive music history experiences, which include behind-the-scenes access to museums, recording studios, and other historic locations.

Tourists may visit institutions devoted to conserving Nashville's musical legacy, such the Country Music Hall of Fame and Museum, which has historical relics and exhibitions on the biggest names in country music.

Certain excursions provide visitors unparalleled access to the recording studios used by well-known musicians, offering a unique window into the process of creating music and the inner workings of the music business.

Visitors of all ages and backgrounds are immersed in an immersive investigation of Nashville's cultural legacy via interactive exhibits and multimedia presentations that bring the city's music history to life.

Finding Legendary Songs and Performers:
Nashville's music history tours provide fascinating insights into the lives of some of the most well-known songs and performers in the area, shedding light on their creative processes and the cultural significance of their output.

Guests may discover the process of creating songs, the sources of inspiration for beloved songs, and the hardships and successes faced by the performers who brought them to life.

Tours may include stops at locations linked to well-known songs and performers, enabling guests to develop a more intimate connection with the music and a greater understanding of its influence on Nashville and beyond.

Nashville's Future Stars: Seeking the Next Great Thing

Talented musicians and composers have always flourished in Nashville, and the city's music culture is still thriving today thanks to a new wave of up-and-coming performers. There's no shortage of talent to find in Nashville, from bands making waves on the local music scene to singer-songwriters entertaining in small venues.

Watch out for the next big thing in Nashville's always changing music industry, whether you're taking in a showcase at a local music festival or exploring the city's underground music culture.

Private Events at Private Locations:

Emerging musicians in Nashville frequently begin their careers by playing tiny, intimate settings like coffee shops, bars, and listening rooms all across the city.

These locations give aspiring musicians and songwriters a stage on which to display their abilities in a laid-back atmosphere that fosters a personal connection between the audience and the music.

Attendees may experience anything from full-band showcases to acoustic singer-songwriter gigs, all of which provide opportunities for discovering new artists and genres.

Songwriter rounds and open mic nights:

In Nashville's music industry, open mic nights and songwriter rounds are well-liked occasions that provide budding musicians a chance to perform their original songs live for an audience.

These gatherings, which are frequently hosted in pubs, cafés, and music venues all around the city, give musicians a positive space to improve their skills and be noticed.

By supporting artists as they take the stage and use music to tell their story, attendees may feel what it's like to discover fresh talent firsthand.

Local Music Exhibitions and Festivals:

Nashville presents several regional music festivals and showcases all year long, showcasing the city's wide range of musical ability and giving up-and-coming musicians a chance to make their mark.

Events like the East Nashville Crawfish Bash, AmericanaFest, and the Nashville Film Festival's Music Program provide performances by up-and-coming musicians alongside well-known performers, providing an opportunity for exploration and discovery.

These gatherings bring together local and international music enthusiasts, fostering a dynamic environment of ingenuity and cooperation that honors Nashville's rich musical history and bright future.

Creative Communities and Collaborative Spaces:

Nashville's creative communities and collaborative spaces serve as a great source of inspiration and support for up-and-coming artists. These groups bring together musicians, songwriters, producers, and other industry experts to exchange ideas and work together on projects.

Aspiring artists can find tools and networking possibilities in co-working spaces, recording studios, and artist collectives. These locations aid in the development of their abilities and assist them negotiate the music industry.

Emerging artists may create relationships, obtain visibility, and discover opportunities to perform for a larger audience by interacting with other musicians and creatives.

Chapter 5

Adventures in Culinary Arts

Restaurant Options in Nashville

Nashville's culinary scene was dominated a few years ago by deep-fried, saucy dishes that might have raced the heart of the healthiest person. For those who enjoyed hearty portions of baked beans, spicy macaroni and cheese, and tender BBQ pork, this southern metropolis was the place to go.

But during the past 10 or so years, Nashville's culinary culture has broadened to include less cholesterol and more international cuisine; popular **Cajun, Indian, Mediterranean, Mexican**, and Italian meals can be found all throughout the city at restaurants. The greatest way to appreciate Nashville's fusion of modern and traditional is through culinary excursions.

For a more relaxed dining experience, try the grilled pork and ribs in the West End. Try the famous Nashville hot chicken at **Hattie B's, Bolton's Spicy Chicken** & Fish, or Prince's Hot Chicken Shack. Coneheads is a contemporary take on a classic dish that serves delicious chicken in waffle cones, making it ideal for grab-and-go meals.

Check out The District for additional upscale dining options. Here, you may enjoy live music while dining at the tapas-focused Black Rabbit or indulge in Cajun food at the Bourbon Street Blues & Boogie Bar. Don't forget to check out the vegan comfort food at Southern V or Butcher & Bee in East Nashville, which features a vegan version of hot chicken! And anytime your sweet tooth strikes, treat yourself to something delicious like Morning Glory Donuts or Mike's Ice Cream.

The city's bar scene is another something you shouldn't overlook. Locals say Mickey's Tavern and Dino's are two of the greatest locations to enjoy a drink in town. If you want to learn more about Nashville's brewing and distillery culture, check out these great locations. If all you want to do is relax with a drink and some live music, you can even go bar hopping down Broadway.

A carefully calibrated paste of cayenne pepper is applied to this hot bird after it has been **marinated, breaded, fried**, and seasoned with a water-based concoction. Depending on your tolerance for heat, this dish will make your taste buds dance or scream. Pickles are typically used to counterbalance the heat in a slice of white bread.

Hot chicken in Nashville is a culinary wonder that entices the senses and tells a fiery tale of revenge that has made the city famous. This hot bird is breaded, deep-fried till crispy, then marinated in a spice concoction based on water.

After that, cayenne paste is generously applied. This recipe will make your taste buds dance—or scream, depending on how much spice you can handle—as it has been precisely calibrated to produce exactly the right amount of heat.

This well-known dish has the perfect balance of flavor and spice, and it's best enjoyed with a slice of white bread with pickles on the side.

Legend has it that **hot chicken** originated in the 1930s when a woman gave her unfaithful boyfriend some really hot chicken in an attempt to reprimand him. He loved it, much to her surprise, and a food star was born.

Hot chicken has now grown to be a beloved local tradition thanks to establishments like **Prince's Hot Chicken Shack**, where it all began, and more recent additions like Hattie B's that are always turning up the heat on this Nashville favorite.

The good news is that **Nashville's spicy chicken** comes in a range of spice levels, from "**mild**" to "so hot you'll drop your pearls and reach for the **milk**." So fear not, adventurous eaters. So whether you're a seasoned spice enthusiast or you prefer milder cuisine, Music City has a spicy chicken experience waiting for you.

When it comes to tasting Nashville's food selections, hot chicken is only the beginning. Food trucks and markets provide a variety of local delicacies and street cuisine that are sure to please even the pickiest eater. There are so many delicious things to sample, from conventional tacos and BBQ to artisanal ice cream and gourmet grilled cheese sandwiches.

So whether you're enjoying hot chicken at a renowned shack or eating street food at a bustling market, Nashville's culinary scene is sure to satisfy your cravings and leave you wanting more. Your palate will be grateful as you go on a delicious journey through Music City's booming food scene!

For those who love barbecue, Nashville's distinctive culinary experience delivers a unique combination of smoky flavors and Southern warmth. Nashville's barbecue tradition, which offers tender, slow-smoked meats paired with delectable sides and sauces, embodies true Southern hospitality.

The foundation of Nashville's **barbecue culture** is a commitment to employing high-quality ingredients and tried-and-true cooking techniques. In the city, pit masters spend hours tending to their smokers in order to extract complex, flavorful scents from cuts of meat like brisket, pulled pig, and ribs. Barbecue that is juicy, tender, and delicious is the ideal result.

It's not just about the meat, though; Nashville's barbecue joints are experts at creating mouthwatering sides and sauces to pair with their smoky creations.

There are many other options to round off your barbecue feast, such as creamy macaroni and cheese or tangy coleslaw and baked beans. Remember to include the sauce as well; Nashville's BBQ joints provide choices that will satisfy any palate, whether it be sweet and sour, spicy and smokey, or somewhere in between.

When it comes to experiencing BBQ heaven, Nashville has no shortage of options. Whether you're searching for a dirt bar without frills or a classy gastropub, the region has barbecue restaurants to suit every taste and budget. Additionally, you can be certain that your experience will be very delicious because the city takes great pride in its BBQ and the pitmasters are masters in their craft.

Whether you're indulging in a sampling platter at a neighborhood BBQ festival or a plate of ribs at your favorite BBQ joint, be ready to experience barbecue nirvana in Music City.

Nashville's BBQ scene will probably leave you wanting more because of its unparalleled hospitality, smoky flavors, and Southern comfort.

Hot and Spicy Chicken:

Step 1: Marinate the chicken.
In a bowl, mix buttermilk, salt, pepper, and any extra spices (paprika, cayenne, and garlic powder).

Chicken parts including thighs, drumsticks, and breasts should be dipped in the buttermilk mixture. Cover and chill for at least 1 hour or overnight.

Step 2: Put on and shut off

In a separate bowl, mix flour with other spices (paprika, cayenne, garlic powder, salt, and pepper).

Dredge each marinated chicken piece in the seasoned flour mixture to coat it evenly.

Deep-fry the chicken after that.

Heat the oil in a large pan or deep fryer to **350°F (175°C).**

To avoid crowding, carefully drop the breaded chicken pieces into the hot oil and fry them in batches if necessary.

Fry the chicken for 12 to 15 minutes, or until golden brown and well cooked, depending on the size of the pieces.

In Step 4, make the hot sauce.

In a small saucepan, melt butter and stir in garlic powder, paprika, cayenne, and salt.

Reduce the heat to low and simmer the sauce for a few minutes, until it becomes thoroughly combined and fragrant.

Step Five: Put the Chicken Under Cover

Once the chicken is cooked, generously brush each piece with the hot sauce mixture to ensure it is evenly covered.

Step Six: Showcase

Serve the hot chicken immediately; it tastes best served warm on a slice of white bread with a side order of pickles to chill it down.

Nashville's Hot Catfish:

First, allow the catfish to marinade.

In a bowl, combine buttermilk, salt, pepper, and any additional spices you choose.

Immerse the catfish fillets in the buttermilk mixture to coat them evenly. Let them marinade in the refrigerator for at least half an hour.

Step 2: Prepare the Coating

In a shallow dish, mix cornmeal, salt, pepper, and other seasonings (such paprika or cayenne pepper).

Step Three: Utilize and Prepare

After removing the marinated catfish fillets from the buttermilk, completely coat them with the spiced cornmeal mixture.

Heat the oil in a skillet over medium-high heat. The pan should be hot before adding the breaded catfish fillets.

The catfish should be cooked through and golden brown after **3–4 minutes** of cooking on each side.

In Step 4, make the hot sauce.

In a small saucepan, heat the butter, cayenne, spicy sauce, and a little pinch of salt.

Once the sauce has warmed through over low heat, remove from the burner.

Step 5: Coat the catfish.

Once the catfish fillets are fried, generously brush each one with the hot sauce mixture to ensure it is well coated.

Step Six: Showcase

Serve the Nashville hot catfish immediately, garnished with fresh parsley or green onions, if desired. Serve with your favorite side dishes, such as kole slaw or cornbread.

With the help of these detailed directions, you should be able to recreate the authentic tastes of Nashville's hot chicken and hot catfish in your own home!

Street Food & Local Specialties at Markets and Food Trucks

Farm-to-table cuisine blends the freshness and flavor of locally obtained ingredients with the traditional flavors of Southern cookery.

Here's a step-by-step recipe for a farm-to-table dish with Southern influences:

Where to Look for Organic Ingredients?

You may get a range of fresh, in-season meats, veggies, and dairy goods at your local farm stand or farmers' market.

Look for products like free-range eggs and pasture-raised meats, as well as crops like maize, okra, leafy greens, sweet potatoes, and heirloom tomatoes.

Set Up Your Plate:

Select dishes that bring out the flavors of the season and showcase how fresh your ingredients are.

Consider classic Southern dishes like shrimp and grits, fried green tomatoes, collard greens, and cornbread in addition to lighter fare like salads and grilled vegetables.

Prepare your ingredients:

Make sure to thoroughly clean and prepare your vegetables and salad greens, removing any dirt or debris.

If you would like, trim, season, and marinade your meats in addition to bringing any dairy products to room temperature.

Start Preparing Food:

Prepare your proteins first; for example, sear fish or grill chicken or steaks.While your meats are cooking, prepare your accompaniments and side dishes. Saute greens with bacon and garlic, roast vegetables with olive oil and herbs, or prepare a pot of creamy sweet potatoes.

Incorporating grains and carbohydrates into your meal preparation is important. Make a batch of stone-ground grits, bake some cornbread, or boil some fresh pasta for a hearty Southern meal.

Arrange and serve on a plate:

Arrange your cooked meats, side dishes, and accompaniments on plates or platters. For flavor, garnish with fresh herbs or citrus zest.

Enjoy an abundance of freshly cooked, Southern-inspired meals with your friends around the table.

Serve your dinner with a refreshing drink, such as sweet tea, lemonade, or a locally brewed craft beer, to fully enjoy the flavors of the season.

You may create a farm-to-table dining experience that celebrates the richness and freshness of locally produced food while paying tribute to the South's rich culinary tradition by using these recommendations. Enjoy the bounty of the season and the sense of accomplishment that arises from knowing where your food comes from!

Exploring **Nashville's food truck and market** scene is a fantastic way to try local delicacies and street food. This is a comprehensive guide to these culinary locations:

Locating Food Trucks

Check out the local food truck gatherings in Nashville, such "**food truck rodeos,**" when several trucks get together to provide a variety of culinary delicacies.

Follow Nashville food truck associations or their social media sites to stay up to date on their locations and schedules.

When you find a food truck that catches your eye, visit it and see what's being served.

Never be afraid to seek guidance from the personnel or inquire about any discounts or in-house delicacies they might be offering.

Trying Cuisine on the Street:

When placing your food truck order, consider ordering a variety of foods so you may sample various flavors.

In Nashville, look for street food staples like gourmet grilled cheese, hot chicken sliders, artisanal ice cream, and BBQ sandwiches.

If you're feeling adventurous, try recipes that call for local ingredients or unique flavor combinations.

Examining the Farmers' Market Area:

Explore the Nashville farmers' markets for an extensive selection of prepared foods, handcrafted goods, and fresh produce.

Come early for the best selection of baked goods, cheeses, meats, seasonal fruits and vegetables, and more.

Take some time to browse the market stalls, talk to the vendors, and check out their products.

Consider purchasing ingredients for a DIY farm-to-table meal at home or selecting pre-made meals for a picnic in the park.

Recognizing and Taking Specialty Areas:

Seek for Nashville-specific favorites like hot chicken, biscuits and gravy, Southern-style barbecue, and fried green tomatoes.

Don't forget to try some of the local specialties, such Goo Goo Clusters,

Nashville hot fish, and Bushwacker beverages.

Don't pass up the opportunity to purchase goods and handcrafted things from small, regional businesses and artisans.

Enjoying the Present:

Street food and farmers' markets provide casual, laid-back dining experiences; take your time and enjoy the atmosphere.

You may increase your chances of uncovering any hidden gems by chatting with other food enthusiasts and inquiring about the products being sold by vendors.

Remember to snap photos of your culinary adventures so you can document your culinary travels throughout Nashville.

By visiting food trucks and markets, you may sample a range of street delicacies and local specialties and enjoy Nashville's flourishing culinary culture. So savor some delicious street cuisine in Music City and be ready to gorge yourself!

Chapter 6

Hotels & Lodging: Suggested Locations to Stay in Nashville

Cozy vacation rentals: a home away from home Affordable alternatives: Reasonably priced hotel choices

WHERE CAN I RESIDE IN NASHVILLE?

Despite being known as **"Music City,"** Nashville, Tennessee, has much more to see and do than just its sounds. Thanks to its many dining options, it has become a favorite destination for foodies searching for the tastiest hot chicken or the heartiest meat-and-threes.

Notable chefs are also upgrading dining options across the city, including venues within some of Nashville's top hotels.

Nashville offers an equal amount of free music from every honky tonk in the city as it does live music venues. With something to suit every taste, Nashville has grown to be a well-liked vacation and entertainment destination.

Many of the best places to stay are situated in the heart of the activity. The outstanding resorts include a friendly staff, a ton of amenities on site, opulent accommodations, and more.

The editors of U.S. News Hotels aggregate and evaluate user evaluations, star ratings, and industry awards every year to create this list of the best hotels. It is the only ranking system that considers feedback from experts and tourists alike.

Hotel Nashville:

Expense: $309 to $432 daily

The rationale for the choice of Hotel Nashville: Conveniently located in the heart of the city, Hotel Nashville offers luxurious accommodations for travelers. Its excellent location and first-rate amenities, which include free Wi-Fi and a nightly resort fee, make it the ideal choice for travelers seeking comfort and convenience while visiting Nashville.

The Joseph, a Luxury Collection Hotel in Nashville:

Cost per night: $339 to $378

Why The Joseph was the choice: The Joseph, a Luxury Collection Hotel, offers an unparalleled level of sophistication and luxury. With a 5-star rating and amenities like fitness centers, pools, and pet-friendly policies, it's the best choice for travelers looking for an opulent and remarkable vacation to Nashville.

Conrad Nashville:

Cost per night: $279 to $287 Motives for Choosing Conrad Nashville Only 0.8 miles from the city center, Conrad Nashville provides a refined and elegant place to stay. With 4.5 stars and complimentary Wi-Fi, it's a fantastic choice for discerning travelers seeking a convenient yet opulent stay in Nashville.

The Hermitage Hotel:

Cost: For a few chosen days, not guaranteed. Just Why Choose The Hermitage? Renowned for its grandeur and timeless elegance, the

Hermitage Hotel is a well-known historical landmark. With a 5-star hotel class, a fitness center, a business center, and pet-friendly regulations, it offers guests a luxurious and exceptional stay in Nashville.

The Kimpton Aertson Hotel:

Price: $289–299 per night Motives for Choosing Kimpton Aertson The chic and dynamic Kimpton Aertson Hotel is a terrific spot to stay in the heart of Nashville. For those searching for a stylish and modern experience in Music City, this is the best choice thanks to its pet-friendly accommodations and 4.5-star hotel class.

Nashville's Thompson

Cost per night: $277 to $285 Motives for Choosing Thompson Nashville With its sleek and modern design, Thompson Nashville offers a polished stay only a short distance from the city's busy downtown area. This 4-star hotel is an excellent choice for individuals looking for more opulent housing in Nashville since it has excellent amenities, a fitness facility, and complimentary Wi-Fi.

The Union Station Nashville Yards Autograph Collection:

Expense: $299 per night

Justification for Choosing The Union Station: Situated in a historic rail station, The Union Station Nashville Yards offers visitors a unique and remarkable Nashville experience. With its 4-star rating, business center, fitness center, and pet-friendly policies, the hotel offers a unique experience by fusing modern amenities with historic charm.

Nashville's Noelle: A Tribute Portfolio Hotel

$313 per night is the cost.

Why Should You Choose Noelle? The Noelle offers a stylish and contemporary location to stay in the heart of downtown Nashville. Thanks to its free Wi-Fi and 4-star hotel classification, it provides visitors with a comfortable and practical base for seeing the city's attractions and nightlife.

The Four Seasons Hotel in Nashville:

Cost: For a few chosen days, not guaranteed. Justification for Choosing Four Seasons: The Four Seasons Hotel Nashville epitomizes luxury and sophistication.

Its 5-star hotel excellence and impeccable service provide guests an unrivaled experience of luxury and comfort right in the heart of Music City.

The JW Marriott Nashville:

Expense: $305 to $312 per evening; Motives for Choosing JW Marriott: The JW Marriott Nashville offers a luxurious and modern stay right in the heart of downtown Nashville. Because of its fitness facility, 4-star hotel class, and convenient location, it's a terrific choice for travelers searching for opulent accomodation and first-rate amenities when visiting Nashville.

Nashville vacation rentals are cozy homes away from homes that may suit a variety of needs and preferences, allowing guests to live like locals in Music City. These rentals, which range from comfortable flats in trendy neighborhoods to spacious mansions in quiet regions, are guaranteed to have something for everyone, whether you are traveling alone, with a companion, in a group, or with your family.

One of the key attractions of Nashville vacation rentals is the feeling of absorption and genuineness they provide. Rather than renting an ordinary hotel room, you may live like a local and tour the city's neighborhoods, dining at local restaurants and shopping at local markets.

Many vacation homes are located in residential districts, making it convenient for guests to enjoy Nashville's daily rhythm and attractions as well as entertainment places.
Furthermore, compared to traditional housing, Nashville vacation rentals provide greater privacy and independence. With fully equipped kitchens, living rooms, and outdoor spaces, guests may enjoy all the

conveniences of home while on vacation. Vacation rentals provide you the room and freedom to tailor your stay to your preferences, whether you want to cook meals for your loved ones, relax in a quiet backyard, or unwind in a comfortable living room after a long day of sightseeing.

Moreover, vacation rentals may be a more cost-effective option for longer stays or larger groups because they often offer lower rates than hotels. Many hosts of vacation rentals are also locals who may offer recommendations and tips for things to do in Nashville, adding an extra special touch of hospitality to your stay.

All things considered, by combining the thrill of travel with the conveniences of home, Nashville vacation rentals provide a unique and wonderful way to see the city.

- **Low-cost Alternatives**: Reasonably Priced Accommodation Options

For those on a limited budget, Nashville offers a range of affordable hotel options that are both handy and pleasant without going over budget. These alternatives ensure that visitors may enjoy Music City without going over their hotel budget by catering to a variety of interests and needs.

One popular low-cost option in Nashville are the several budget motels and hotels that are dispersed across the city. Travelers on a tight budget who appreciate affordability without sacrificing amenities like complimentary breakfast, parking, and Wi-Fi will love these accommodations. Generally speaking, they offer affordable, well-kept accommodations.

Nashville Downtown Hostel:

This hostel offers reasonably priced dorm-style accommodation with shared bathrooms and common areas, conveniently located in the heart of downtown Nashville. Visitors may enjoy complimentary breakfast, free Wi-Fi, and scheduled events including pub crawls and live music performances.

A communal kitchen, a lounge room, laundry facilities, and luggage storage are among the amenities. The front desk is manned around-the-clock.

Prices: $25 to $40 per night, on average.

In Music City, a little house

This reasonably priced housing option gives you the opportunity to live in Nashville like a little house. The cozy little home features a modest but usable kitchen, a separate bathroom, and a sleeping loft. Situated in a quiet neighborhood close to city attractions, guests may enjoy a peaceful retreat.

Facilities include free parking, a kitchenette, a private bathroom, and an outside dining area.

$60 - $80 per night is the price range.

Guesthouse East Nashville:

Description: Located in East Nashville, this quaint guesthouse provides reasonably priced individual rooms with common facilities. Visitors may take use of the shared kitchen, unwind in the cozy lounge area, and get free coffee and tea. A short stroll from the guesthouse brings you to hip eateries, concert halls, and retail stores.

Free Wi-Fi, a living space, a shared kitchen, and restrooms are among the amenities.

$50 - $70 per night is the price range.

Nashville's Pod Hotel:

Drawing inspiration from the idea of pod-style lodging, this low-cost hotel provides small yet practical rooms equipped with contemporary conveniences. Each pod has a cozy bed, a designated storage area, and individual charging ports. There is a rooftop patio with city views, a community kitchen, and shared restrooms for guests to use.

Amenities include a rooftop patio, free Wi-Fi, a shared kitchen, and restrooms.

Cost: $40 to $60 per night.

Memphis Micro-Loft:

This micro-loft in downtown Nashville is a great place for singles or couples looking for a comfortable and reasonably priced place to stay. The modern yet modest loft has a separate bathroom, a small kitchenette, and a comfy bed. Convenient self-check-in options and access to a shared rooftop terrace are available to visitors.

Features include a rooftop balcony, a private bathroom, a kitchenette, and complimentary Wi-Fi.

Range of Prices: $70 to $90 per night.

The Music City Motel

Description: Located just outside of Nashville's downtown, this straightforward hotel provides affordable lodging. The hotel offers tidy, cozy rooms with standard conveniences including a microwave, mini-fridge, and TV. Visitors may benefit from easy access to neighboring sites and free parking.

Facilities include air conditioning, a mini-fridge, a microwave, and free parking.

$50 - $70 per night is the price range.

Backpackers Hostel in Nashville:

This hostel, which caters to tourists on a tight budget, offers communal restrooms and common spaces along with dormitory-style guestrooms. In addition to using the shared kitchen and lounging in the lounge area, guests may take part in planned events like movie nights and group excursions.

Free Wi-Fi, a living space, a shared kitchen, and restrooms are among the amenities.

$20 - $30 per night is the price range.

Attractive Cottage in Germantown's History:

Situated in the Germantown section of Nashville, this quaint home provides reasonably priced lodging options for individuals or couples on a budget. The cottage has a tiny kitchenette, a private bathroom, and a cozy bedroom. Visitors may take advantage of the neighborhood's peace and quiet while remaining near the city attractions.

Includes a kitchenette, a private bathroom, a sitting space outside, and complimentary WiFi.

$60 - $80 per night is the price range.

Apartment in Urban Oasis Studio:

This inexpensive studio apartment in downtown Nashville provides a handy and cost-effective place to stay. The studio has a separate bathroom, bedroom space, and well-equipped kitchenette. The building's amenities, which include a rooftop terrace, fitness facility, and common lounge, are available to guests.

Facilities include a rooftop patio, workout center, kitchenette, and private bathroom.

Range of Prices: $70 to $90 per night.

Suburban Retreat in Nashville:

Description: Take a cheap suburban getaway to get away from the bustle of Nashville's downtown. The guest suite, which has a separate entrance, bedroom, bathroom, and sitting space, provides cozy lodging in a peaceful residential neighborhood.

Visitors may take advantage of the quiet neighborhood and quick access to neighboring parks and attractions.

Features include a living room, bedroom, bathroom, and free parking.

$50 - $70 per night is the price range.

Chapter 7

Transportation

How to Get to Nashville

Navigating Nashville

Having a car is the greatest way to navigate about Nashville. Although the city has public transit, it might be challenging to visit several locations in one day due to the dispersed nature of the districts and attractions.

If you enjoy riding, you may also benefit from BCycle, a network of electric bike stations located around the city. Another effective way to visit the city is via bus, which is used by many of the best guided excursions in the area.

Rent a Car:

Having a vehicle rental gives you the freedom to see Nashville at your own speed. Free parking is available at many hotels, and parking in the downtown area is easy to locate, while street meters may require change. There are rental car companies at Nashville International Airport as well as all across the city.

Advice: For information on parking, including an interactive map and discounted prices in downtown Nashville, see the city's website.

MTA Public Bus System:

Nashville's public bus system travels all around the city and has an express route that goes straight to and from the airport. The cost of a fare is reasonable, at about $2 each ride. For unlimited rides throughout your visit, think about getting a seven-day pass **($20 for adults and $10 for children).**

If you want to take the bus regularly, use the seven-day pass for easy and affordable commuting.

Services for Taxis:

For short travels or while going to and from the airport, metered taxis are an easy and speedy mode of transportation. A cab from the Nashville airport to the city center will cost you about $25 flat. In and around Nashville, ride-hailing services like Uber and Lyft are also operational.

Although cabs are often accessible, it might be more convenient to explore different districts and sites with your own car.

BCycle: Rental Bicycles:

With an electric bike from BCycle, tour Nashville's streets and beautiful surroundings. For quick journeys or longer excursions, you may hire a bike from stations that are conveniently placed all around the city. A single admission costs $5 per thirty minutes, while a three-day pass costs $25 and allows for unlimited rides for 120 minutes.

Advice: Make the most of biking's adaptability and environmental benefits to find hidden treasures and popular destinations nearby.

Whether you like the freedom of a rental vehicle, the ease of public transit, or the rush of bicycling, Nashville has a variety of ways to get about its busy streets and interesting sights. *Select the means of transportation that most closely matches your schedule, then take pleasure in easily visiting Music City.*

DIRECTIONS TO NASHVILLE

The primary entry point into the city is **Nashville International Airport (BNA),** which is well situated southeast of Nashville's downtown. Here's additional specific information about arriving to BNA via plane:

Airport Amenities: To improve visitors' experiences, Nashville International Airport provides a number of amenities and services. These include of several food establishments, stores, lounges, and facilities like free Wi-Fi all across the airport.

Flights to Domestic and International Locations: BNA offers connections to both domestic and foreign locations. Major American cities are served by domestic planes, which often travel to hubs like

Atlanta, Chicago, and Dallas. With a few flights to Europe and other locations, international flights mostly go to locations in the Caribbean, Canada, and Mexico.

Airlines: Nashville International Airport serves a large number of airlines that provide a variety of flight options. Both local and international connection is offered by major carriers including American Airlines, Delta Air Lines, Southwest Airlines, and United Airlines.

Price Range: The cost of airfare from Nashville International Airport varies based on a number of variables, such as the airline selected, the departure location, and the time of booking. Domestic flight costs normally range from **$100 to $500** or more, while international flight costs can vary from several hundred to over a thousand dollars, contingent upon the route and class of travel.

Booking Advice: It's ideal to book your flights well in advance to get the best deals, especially during holidays or popular travel periods. To get the best deals, take into account variable trip dates and evaluate costs from several airlines and online booking services.

Go Requirements: Make sure your passport is valid for at least six months after the day you want to go abroad. Make sure you are aware of the precise criteria for your trip well in advance. Certain countries may additionally require a visa or other entrance paperwork.

A *government-issued ID,* such as a driver's license or passport card, is usually adequate for domestic flights inside the United States.

Nashville International Airport is a great option for both local and foreign tourists since it provides easy access to the city and its surrounding attractions.

Chapter 8

Nashville's Festivals & Events

Honoring the Arts, Music, and Cuisine

Nashville's calendar is jam-packed with festivals and events that highlight the vibrant energy and wide range of cultural options available in the city. There's always something going on in Music City, from music festivals honoring the city's rural beginnings to food events showcasing its Southern cuisine.

Fans of country music from all over the world come together for the four days of the CMA Music Festival to enjoy live performances, fan interactions, and events with famous people. The Music City Food +

Wine Festival, which brings together renowned chefs, artisanal producers, and beverage specialists to tantalize taste buds, provides food fans a scrumptious presentation of Nashville's culinary culture.

CMA Music Festival:

Date: Usually takes place in June every year. One of the biggest country music festivals in the world, this four-day affair brings people to Music City from all over the world. Top country musicians will perform live, and there will be fan interactions, autograph signings, and other activities.

Location: Nashville's downtown stages and Nissan Stadium, among other locations.

Food & Wine Festival in Music City:

Date: September is when it usually happens. This event, which brings together renowned chefs, restaurants, artisanal producers, and beverage experts for a weekend of food and wine tastings, cooking demos, panel discussions, and live music, honors Nashville's burgeoning culinary industry.

Venue: Usually hosted in State Park's Bicentennial Capitol Mall as well as other venues across the city.

Nashville International Film Festival:

Date: Usually takes place in October.

Featuring independent films from all over the world, the Nashville Film Festival is one of the biggest and oldest film festivals in the US. It includes panel discussions, seminars, and networking opportunities in addition to the screenings of documentaries, animated films, shorts, and feature films.

Location: A number of theaters and locations across Nashville, such as the Main Venue of the Nashville Film Festival and the Regal Hollywood Theaters.

Shakespeare Festival in Nashville:

Date: Usually occurs throughout the summer.

This festival honors William Shakespeare's literary contributions by presenting his plays in expert performances that showcase their inventive and distinctive approaches. It consists of community outreach projects, educational courses, and outdoor concerts.

Venue: Depending on the production, Centennial Park or other outdoor areas.

Cherry Blossom Festival in Nashville:

Date: Usually takes place in April.

Description: Featuring cherry blossom viewing, traditional Japanese music and dance performances, art exhibits, food sellers, and cultural demonstrations, this yearly event honors Japanese culture and the approach of spring. It seeks to enhance friendship and cross-cultural understanding between the US and Japan.

Location: Public Square Park in Nashville and the surrounding surroundings are the festival's locations.

Festival of Americana Music:

Date: Typically, September is the date.

The Americana Music Festival honors the rich legacy of American roots music, encompassing rock, folk, country, and blues. Together with panel discussions, workshops, and networking opportunities for professionals in the music industry, it offers live performances by both established and up-and-coming musicians.

Location: Several locations across Nashville, such as outdoor stages, clubs, and historic theaters.

Nashville Pride Festival:

Date: Usually takes place in June.

Description: Throughout the course of a weekend filled with live performances, drag acts, vendor booths, food trucks, and local resources, this festival honors and promotes Nashville's LGBTQ+ community. A vibrant procession through Nashville's downtown is part of the festivities, which also feature musical acts and kid-friendly events.

Location: Public Square Park and the adjacent streets in Nashville's downtown are the site of the event.

Festival of Tomato Art:

Date: Typically, August is the date.

The Tomato Art Festival is a unique and enjoyable occasion that honors everything associated with tomatoes, encompassing art, cuisine, music, and culture. A parade, live music, art exhibits with tomato themes, competitions, cooking demos, and a wide selection of tomato-based foods from neighborhood eateries and food sellers are all part of the festivities.

Location: The East Nashville neighborhood of Five Points is the site of the event.

Chapter 9

Practical Information

LANGUAGE AND COMMUNICATION TIPS

Since English is the primary language in Nashville, the majority of people and businesses will speak it while interacting. But because of Nashville's multicultural population, you can run into folks who speak various languages, particularly in neighborhoods with a lot of visitors or foreign residents.

The following linguistic and communication hints can help you get about Nashville:

Since English is the language that most people in Nashville speak, it helps to be at least somewhat conversant in the language for communication needs.

If you struggle with basic English conversation, think about keeping a translation app on your phone.

When interacting with natives who might speak a different language, use patience and consideration. Speaking properly and gently can help both sides understand each other better.

Finances: Money and Modes of Payment:
It's vital to comprehend the accepted forms of payment and money in Nashville to ensure a seamless and trouble-free trip.

What you should know is as follows:

Currency: The US Dollar **(USD)** is the currency used in Nashville and the rest of the United States. It is advised to carry some cash on hand in case of minor transactions and purchases.

Payment Options: Major credit and debit cards, including Visa, Mastercard, American Express, and Discover, are accepted across Nashville. But it's always a good idea to have some cash on hand as well, particularly for smaller companies or restaurants that might not take credit or debit cards.

WAYS TO PRESERVE MONEY IN NASHVILLE

Most downtown hotels in Nashville are conveniently located for travelers to stroll to major music destinations such as **"honky-tonk row"** on Broadway.

In the past, Nashville, Tennessee, was exclusively home to artists and songwriters eager to sign the next big record contract. However, everything has changed. The airport is crowded with tourists from all around the world today.

Given its ascent to **"It City"** reputation, it should come as no surprise that Music City has emerged as one of the most popular vacation destinations for music enthusiasts, bachelorette parties, and astute tourists. It might also be a reasonably priced destination provided you do your research before leaving.

You don't have to empty your bank account to take advantage of all that Music City has to offer. U.S. News asked the concierges of some of the best hotels in the area for ideas. Discover the greatest methods to save money by using a few pointers from these knowledgeable locals.

Get free live music to listen to.
You may be shocked to hear that you don't even need to open your checkbook to enjoy live music in Nashville year-round.

Spending time at the downtown honky-tonks is one of the finest ways to experience the city on a tight budget. The majority of the music establishments along the strip provide free live music, featuring both established musicians and up-and-coming artists.

Andrew Atkins III, a lifelong local and lead navigator/concierge at the Renaissance Nashville Hotel, adds, "Unlike cities that are not Nashville, guests are not paying a cover charge to do the honky-tonks on Broadway."

"So, there you have it—a savings. Where else could you get the type of entertainment we offer starting at noon every day for, who knows, $10 or $20?"

In case you're not like country music, you should know that Nashville boasts a very varied music culture. Says Atkins, "We're not Country Music City, we're Music City."

Nashville's Public Square Park, a 2-acre green area in the center of downtown, hosts a live music series for tourists seeking for something a bit different.
The lineup for Lightning 100's Live on the Green Music Festival includes singer-songwriters and indie rock bands. Past performers include Rodrigo y Gabriela, Elle King, Ben Harper & The Innocent Criminals, and the Cold War Kids.

"Live on the Green is absolutely amazing," says Hilton Nashville Downtown concierge Dawn Kote. Grammy Award winners are on the roster. It's also free. It takes place in the latter part of August and the first few weeks of September. It's the most underappreciated music series in the nation, in my opinion."

Think carefully about where you stay.

Consider your activities while in town before making your hotel reservations. Make plans to reserve a hotel that is close to some of the attractions on your list of things to do. In this manner, you may be able to reduce the amount of Uber trips you take and maybe avoid renting a car altogether.

"Be mindful of what is accessible by foot.

"Try to locate yourself in close proximity to some of your favorite activities," advises

Kelcie Borton, the Sheraton Grand Nashville Downtown's head concierge.

Nashville has the advantage of having a large number of its most well-liked attractions situated downtown. From most downtown hotels, it's an easy stroll to the Ryman Auditorium, the Country Music Hall of Fame and Museum, and "honky-tonk row" on Broadway.

Speak with your concierge.
In addition to assisting with transportation arrangements, concierges can provide suggestions for activities to do while visiting the area. Additionally, they may typically assist you in avoiding paying excessive prices for tickets at nearby sites.

Check to discover whether your hotel offers a concierge if you're looking to cut costs.

Head concierge at the Hutton Hotel Laura Cunningham said, "We might be able to help you get service fees waived." You may even be eligible for a discount with your hotel key. Visit visitmusiccity.com.au. It also offers a ton of discounts and coupons."

Benefit from the MTA Music City Circuit in Nashville.

The Nashville Music City Circuit, a free bus route for locals and visitors alike, makes stops at most of the major downtown attractions, such as the Frist Center for the Visual Arts, the Ryman Auditorium, the Country Music Hall of Fame and Museum, and the Schermerhorn Symphony Center.

Adam Chantarumporn, a celebrity concierge at the Gaylord Opryland Resort & Convention Center, states that "it's a full loop around downtown." **"You can get a full tour of downtown."**

On weekdays, the Nashville Music City Circuit is open from 6:30 a.m. to 11 p.m., and on weekends, it is open from 11 a.m. to 11 p.m.

Rather of having dinner, treat yourself to a fancy meal.

There weren't many eating alternatives in Nashville years ago. However, there has been a gastronomic resurgence in Music City recently. Several of the top chefs in the country have moved here to build restaurants featuring bold and creative dishes.

Rather than merely battered and fried, you're more likely to encounter organic and locally produced ingredients in restaurants across town.

Even with a tight budget, you can still sample some of the best the area has to offer if you're an adventurous gourmet.

"I would advise guests to dine at some of our upscale establishments, but only for lunch! If you go there for lunch instead of dinner, you'll receive more value for your money, according to Kote.

Visitor Health and Safety Advice:

It is crucial to make sure you are safe and healthy while in Nashville. The following comprehensive advice will help you make sure you're safe and well while visiting:

Drink plenty of water since Nashville's summers are hot and muggy and frequently reach high temperatures. Drinking lots of water throughout the day is essential to staying hydrated, especially if you're spending time outside taking in the sights of the city or going to outdoor activities.

Sun Protection: Wear sunglasses to protect your eyes, a wide-brimmed hat to shade your face and neck, and sunscreen with a high SPF rating to protect yourself from the sun's damaging rays. Make sure you often reapply sunscreen, particularly if you're swimming or perspiring.

Precautions for Safety: Although tourists can feel quite safe in Nashville, it is still important to exercise common sense. Steer clear of uncharted territory or dimly lit regions on foot, especially at night.

In busy streets or popular tourist places, especially, be mindful of your surroundings and take precautions to keep your valuables safe.

Emergency Services: Become familiar with the phone numbers and emergency contacts of the local police, fire, and medical departments. In an emergency, phone 911 to get help right away. Having a list of local hospitals or urgent care facilities on hand is also a smart idea in case you need medical help.

COVID-19 Precautions: Because of the continuing COVID-19 pandemic, it's critical to abide by advised health protocols in order to stop the virus from spreading. In addition to social distance and often washing your hands with soap and water or using hand sanitizer, you should wear masks in busy outdoor places and interior public venues.

(IF NECESSARY,BECAUSE COVID IS A FIASCO BY PASTOR CHRIS OYAHKILOME DSC Dd Dd)

You may have a worry-free trip to Nashville and maximize your time experiencing the dynamic culture and attractions of the city by adhering to these health and safety recommendations.

Practical Apps and Maps to Help Visitors Explore Nashville There are a number of practical applications and maps that may make traveling across Nashville easier. The following maps and applications are suggested:

Google Maps: Turn-by-turn instructions, up-to-date traffic information, and comprehensive maps are all available in this flexible navigation tool. It may be used to plan routes and determine travel times, as well as to locate hotels, restaurants, and other sites of interest in Nashville.

Lyft/Uber: If you don't have access to a car or would rather not drive, ride-hailing services like Lyft and Uber are practical choices for traveling around Nashville. All you have to do is use the app to request a ride, and a driver will come pick you up and transport you to your location.

Nashville MTA: The Metropolitan Transit Authority (MTA) app offers details about bus routes, timetables, and ticket prices for the city's public transit system. It allows you to use your smartphone to buy tickets, plan your route, and monitor bus arrivals in real time.

BCycle: If you're an avid cyclist, you can find and unlock electric bikes at stations all across Nashville using the BCycle app. The app allows you to track the length and distance of your ride, locate available bikes, and verify station locations and availability.

The official tourist guide to Nashville, the Visit Music City app, provides insider information, event schedules, restaurant suggestions, and much more. With its help, you may explore areas, find upcoming events like concerts and festivals, and make custom itineraries depending on your interests.

Nashville Parks Finder: The Nashville Parks Finder app offers details about the city's parks, greenways, and leisure centers to outdoor enthusiasts. It allows you to look up parks in your neighborhood, see maps of nearby trails, and find out about features like sports fields, playgrounds, and picnic spots.

You can easily explore Nashville and make the most of your visit to this dynamic and lively city by utilizing these apps and maps.

Chapter 10

Conclusion

My Nashville Experience: Final Thoughts and Reflections

I feel content and grateful as I take a seat back and think back on my stay in Nashville. My time in Music City has been nothing short of amazing, full with life-changing events, enlightening encounters, and insightful learning opportunities. I can't help but think back on the wide range of feelings and insights that have followed me as I say goodbye to this dynamic and alluring city.

Nashville has certainly lived up to its status as the "**Music City**," as it is sometimes referred to. I've been engrossed in the soul-stirring tunes and rhythms that echo through its streets, from the recognizable honky-tonks dotting Broadway to the famed Ryman Auditorium. Every live performance, whether by established performers or up-and-coming ones, has deeply impacted me and served as a constant reminder of the ability of music to bring people together, inspire, and elevate.

However, Nashville is more than simply its music—it's a creative, culinary, and cultural hotspot. From the bohemian vibes of East Nashville to the urban beauty of The Gulch, the city's unique tapestry of art, architecture, and food enthralled me as I strolled around its eclectic districts.

Experiences have provided a window into Nashville's rich cultural legacy, from relishing the spicy tastes of hot chicken to touring the iconic sites that dot the cityscape.

Furthermore, my trip around Nashville has served as evidence of the kind and welcoming nature of its citizens. I've been greeted with wide arms and accepted as a member of the Nashville family, whether I'm talking to people on a guided tour or laughing with other tourists at a local café.

These exchanges and relationships have given my trips more depth and significance and served as a constant reminder of the ability of human connection to cross boundaries and create enduring memories.

I have a wealth of memories, insights, and lessons from my time in Nashville that will stick with me long after I leave its busy streets behind as I get ready to say goodbye. From the surreal highs of attending live events to the reflective times spent in its beautiful parks, Nashville has deeply impacted my spirit and shaped who I am in ways I never could have predicted.

To sum up, my time in Nashville has been incredibly altering. It's a city that has rekindled my love for music, expanded my views, and served as a constant reminder of the joys of traveling and experiencing new things.

I'm leaving Music City with a fresh appreciation for its enchantment and the enormous influence it has had on my life as I make my way back home. Thank you,

Nashville, for the experiences, songs, and memories that I will always cherish. Goodbye, but not farewell, till we cross paths again.

THANKS FOR READING, GET MORE OF YOUR TRAVEL GUIDES ON INSIDER TRIP AUTHOR CENTERAL PAGE

Made in the USA
Las Vegas, NV
11 April 2024

88567090R00085